For [...] with [...] wishes, [...] (handwritten)

'Authentic and moving poems [...] diate history ... The impression this book [...] ctive talent compelled towards elliptical intensities of insight by the violence in the streets.'
Robert Nye, *THE IRISH PRESS*

'Padraic Fiacc is not an easy poet. He constructs his poems with scrupulous craftsmanship, weighing every syllable. He suppresses the connections of normal narrative, and leaves the reader to supply them for himself.

'Even the way the words lie on the page and the spaces in between are part of their significance. For it is the control of the words, and their placing which controls his deep emotion, modulating his bitterness, his pity ... For me the poet is saying that our troubles are complicated, confused and that their only possible solution calls for the hard disciplines of tolerance and the supreme courage of compassion.'
John Hewitt, *THE BELFAST TELEGRAPH*

'Fiacc is a tough-minded, sensitive poet of painfully bleak awarenesses. And in Fiacc's writing the loss of the Gaelic purity is not allowed to sentimentalise republican militarism or to glamorise violence ... To be Irish in *By The Black Stream* is to know a permanent condition of loss: in *Odour Of Blood* it is to know unending psychic pain. The one is a vision of poignancy sensitively presented, the other of anguish confronted directly with moral and aesthetic courage ...'
Terence Brown, *NORTHERN VOICES*

26 XI 79 (handwritten)

PADRAIC FIACC

Nights in the bad place

Images by Deborah Brown

Blackstaff Press

Published by Blackstaff Press Limited, 16 Donegall Square South, Belfast BT1 5JF with the assistance of the Arts Council of Northern Ireland.

ISBN 0 85640 111 0

Printed by Belfast Litho Printers Limited.

Contents

ACKNOWLEDGEMENTS

Some of the poems in this volume, which was prepared with the assistance
of a Northern Ireland Arts Council Bursary, have already appeared in *New
Poetry 1; The Irish Times; The Irish Press; Hibernia; The Capuchin Annual;
Phoenix; Rann; Threshold; Ten Irish Poets; Irish Poets 1924-1974; The
Wearing of the Black; Odour of Blood* and *By the Black Stream.*

Images by Deborah Brown   Photographs by Sean Waters

'All things are taken from us and become
Portions and parcels of the dreadful Past.'

Tennyson (Lotos-Eaters)

'Why this is hell, nor am I out of it.'

Christopher Marlowe (Doctor Faustus)

for John Marshall,
comrade *en enfer*.

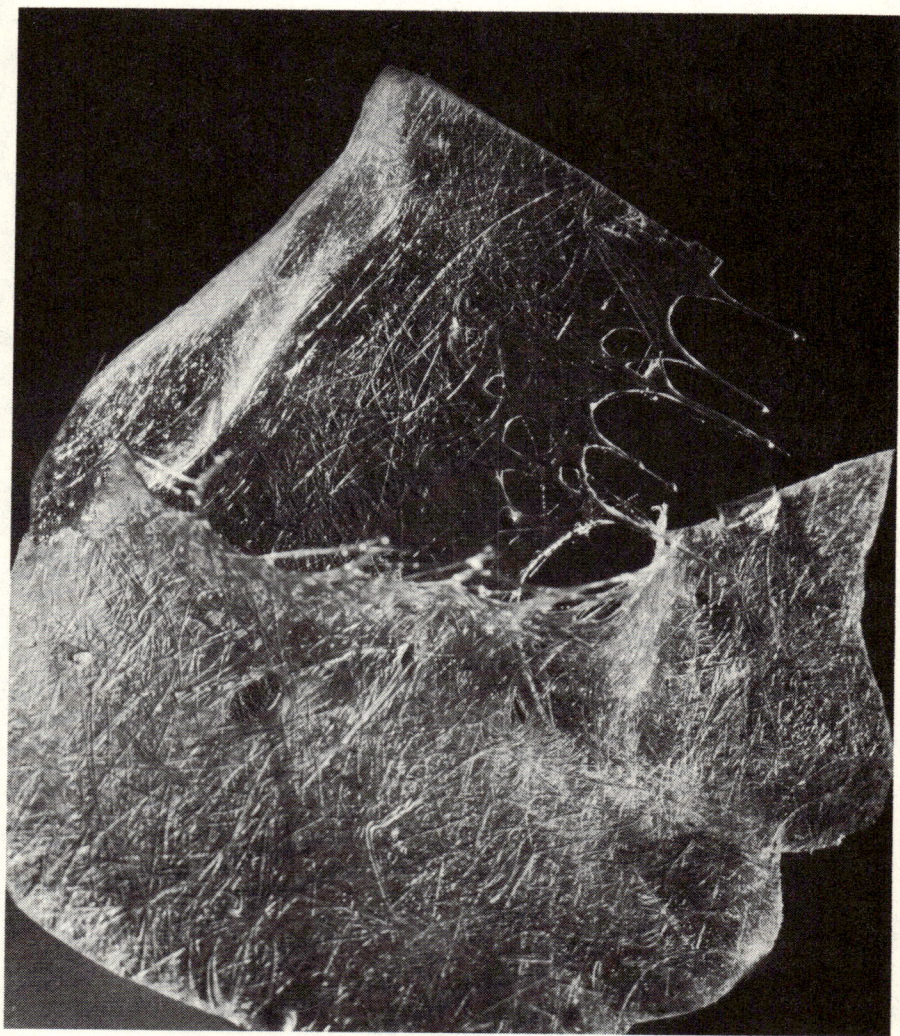

Shadow, Love
for Henry and Mairéad

I wait and you will come
Be it you are a bit late

And we will move back from here

Like the tidal wave
From the earthquake

And be the old use
Of the word 'brave'

And a birthful childhood
                              grave make
For the burnt bee
And the baited sparrow

And bell for the felled

Monastery and a fresh
Childhood home sow

And save grass from the sun by
Depths of origin of
Our two made into one

Shadow, love.

Against Oncoming Civil War
for Brendan and Joan

Salmon silvering grey to die
The summers of the past day

Trapped in our own shallow chill
Shadows, then slowly a whole season's

Twilight bleeds like a blue blood's at
The least scathing, opens out

The silk cloud's spider-fingering pine
Against the going away to sea sky

Cannot be wrenched back nor hoarded
But given only as the black ever-

greens go on living high up over
The mountain hill wall, high up over

This little mill town, the mornings
Getting darker than sundown.

The British Connection

In Belfast, Europe, your man
Met the Military come to raid
The house:

      'Over my dead body
Sir,' he said, brandishing
A real-life sword from some
Old half forgotten war . . .

And youths with real bows and arrows
And coppers and marbles good as bullets

And old time thrupenny bits and stones
Screws, bolts, nuts, (Belfast confetti)

And kitchen knives, pokers, Guinness tins
And nail-bombs down by the Shore Road

And guns under the harbour wharf
And bullets in the docker's tea tin
And gelignite in the tool shed
And grenades in the scullery larder
And weed killer and sugar
And acid in the french letter

And sodium chlorate and nitrates
In the suburban garage
In the boot of the car

And guns in the oven grill
And guns in the spinster's shift

And ammunition and more more
Guns in the broken down rusted
Merry-go-round in the scrap yard

Almost as many hard-on
Guns as there are union jacks.

A Slight Hitch
March 1972

We wanted to think it was the quarry
but the pigeons roared with the white
smoke, black smoke, and the ghost

faced boy-broadcaster
fresh from the scene, broke down
into quivering lips and wild

tears, (can you imagine, and him
'live' on the TV screen!)

had to be quickly replaced
so that the News could be announced
in the usual cold, acid
and dignified way by the

NORTHERN IRELAND BRITISH
BROADCASTING CORPORATION.

Explosion

In the wrong of being
Too broken to know
Or hate what hit them

As Irish as the perpetrator/victim

Broken glass and brickwork eyes
Of police and army chiefs — spin

Suddenly dazed into human beings
Caught out of their British
Army uniform disguise

Are suddenly 'vulnerable'
Are suddenly 'one of us':
                                    born
Thrown to the ground with children screaming
'What is it mommy?
O mommy, what is it?'

Intimate Letter 1973

Our Paris part of Belfast has
Decapitated lamp posts now. Our meeting
Place, the Book Shop, is a gaping
Black hole of charred timber.

Remember that night with you, in
-valided in the top room when
They were throwing petrol bombs through
The windows of catholics, how
My migraine grew to such
A pitch, Brigid said 'Mommy,
I think Daddy is going to burst!'

We all run away from each other's
Particular hell. I didn't
Survive you and her thrown
To the floor when they blew up the Co
-Op at the bottom of the street or Brigid
Waking screaming after this
Or that explosion. Really,
I was the first one to go:

It was I who left you . . .

Saint Coleman's Song For Flight
for Nancy and Brigid — flown

Run like rats from the plague in you.
Before death it is no virtue to be dead.
The crannog in the water, anywhere at all sure!
It is no virtue and it is not nature
To wait to writhe into the ground.

Not one in the Bible could see these dead
Packed on top of the other like dung
Not the two Josephs in Egypt
But would not run!

And Christ's blessing follow
(Is it not a blessing to escape storm?)

Pray to old Joseph not a witless man
Who had the brains not to want to die

But when his time came only and at home in bed,
The door shut on the world, that wolf outside
Munching the leper's head . . .

Orange Man
for Norman Dugdale

The sparrow and the bluetit eating
Greased potato skins are chased

By the blackbird. He's chased by
His own brown mate. She's chased

By a shell-in-beak stone-banging
Puffed out Norwegian thrush that

A gang of tough looking starlings
Easily chases until a shrewd eyed

Navy blue jackdaw, the brute size
Of a graveyard raven invades

The territory that the tiny orange
Breasted robin only thinks is all

His own garden, just can't get let
To stay that dead lonely in.

14

Enemy Encounter
for Lilac

Dumping (left over from the autumn)
Dead leaves, near a culvert
I come on
                    a British Army Soldier
With a rifle and a radio
Perched hiding. He has red hair.

He is young enough to be my weenie
-bopper daughter's boy-friend.
He is like a lonely little winter robin.

We are that close to each other, I
Can nearly hear his heart beating.

I say something bland to make him grin,
But his glass eyes look past my side
-whiskers down
                    the Shore Road street.
I am an Irish man
                    and he is afraid
That I have come to kill him.

Kids at War

i

Irish kids sneer and jeer
At, salute with cat
Calls the dead body
Of the young British soldier

Gave up his life to save
The Irish women and kids

Caught in the Spring
-field Road Barracks
About to explode . . .

ii

The half-kid British soldier
On Lollipop Duty day
Strolls
Into the sweet shop to buy
The Irish kids ice-lollies
Is shot dead
By an Irish kid
Waiting outside
(The one whose head
He rolled his cap on).

'Wee Fellas'

i   The Snatch

It seemed such a cheap
Stage effect of reality that Death
Hiding in the wings
On a foundry roof
Sniping at soldiers, should
Like a childless woman,
Snatch away
A wee chalk-faced boy
Playing marbles in the mud.

ii   Gloria

Glory be to, so
Much for, salute
All us 'armies of

16

The people' who
Drag away
A 'backward boy'

The eldest of a large
Family in the Low
Markets, sentenced to
Reform-school gaols

For being mental
For being poor
For being tortured into
Yelling 'Yes/No,
I am an "informer!" '

And crucify him with
Bullets for nails

Up by the Zoo.

'Wee Girls'

i Enemies

At the Gas and Electric
                    Offices
Black boats with white sails
Float down the stairs
Frighten the five year old
Wee protestant girls.

'Nuns, nuns,' one of them yells
'When are yez gon' to git
                    morried?'

ii   Victory On Ship Street

A bomb-blasted pub!

Another blow struck
For our very own
                    corner
On Devils' Island . . .

Stabbed a thousand
Times by flying glass

Two wee girls in
Hallowe'en dress
                    burnt
To death as witches!

The Black and the White
for Gerald Dawe

Sinking on iron streets, the bin-lid
-shielded, battleship-grey-faced kids

Shinny up the lamp post, cannot tear
Themselves away, refuse to come in

From the dying lost day they douse
With petrol and set the town's holy

Cows on fire, as if the burning bus
                              or car
Could light up their eyes ever, much less
The burning of our own kitchen houses

Coming over the tv screen had held
Any surprises, for really, we wallow in
                              this old
Time western where the 'savages' are bad
And lost the war because the white men

Always have to be the Good Guys.

Tears
for Joseph Parker

i   Unisex

After the bombing the British soldier
Looks up into the barbwired Irish
Twilight. His unflinching open eyes
Deaden, yet involuntarily flood
With the colour of tea
Drenches his combat jacket sleeve.

Now he is hugging,
Now he is giving
                his male love
To a screaming fellow being he does
Not know if it is a man or a woman.

ii   Rape Of The Child

Nine years of age on the bus like a baby
Inside of her crying
Like the length of a life time journey . . .

Not that she 'lost' her penny
But that it was 'stolen' . . .

The Conductor said 'Quit blurtin' love!
Didn't I let you on without the penny?
A penny isn't worth the blurtin' for.'

But nobody can stop the long thin crying

For nobody saw her the day that the men
Were that busy holding back the women
They forgot about the kids

The day she ran up the street alone
To the still smouldering (like peat) pub:

Somebody younger than nine years of age
Watching them dig from the wreckage.

iii Lullaby

When the ricocheting bullet bites into
The young child wanted to walk
In her mother's high heels to push
The doll's pram, she
Gives out a funny little 'oooh!'

And lets the blood spill
All over her bright new bib . . .

No pallbearers are needed.

The young father is able himself to carry
The immaculate white coffin but
Stains it with a dirtyfaced boy's
Fist-smudged tears
                    then suddenly cries
Out like a man being tortured by water.

Black Hole

*A mental illness gives 'X' a youthful
appearance; he's mistaken by the Military
for a youth and dragged to the Barracks*

Eyes running together
Want to, screaming, meet
Each other, forge and fuse
Into one
Head-splitting frown
Cannot shut: I am
This wild wide open
Hysterical as a woman
Man.

Someone kicks me in
'The Temple of
The Holy Ghost' and when
I fall, pees
Across my eyes
(shut hard tight as
a dead bird's).

The RUC man says
'For Christ's sake
He's over forty!'
Would guard
Me against a colour
Of black I never
Believed existed.

Sometimes when I waken
From a nightmare of being
Dead now
There is no God
At this end of that
Black. No God, no man,

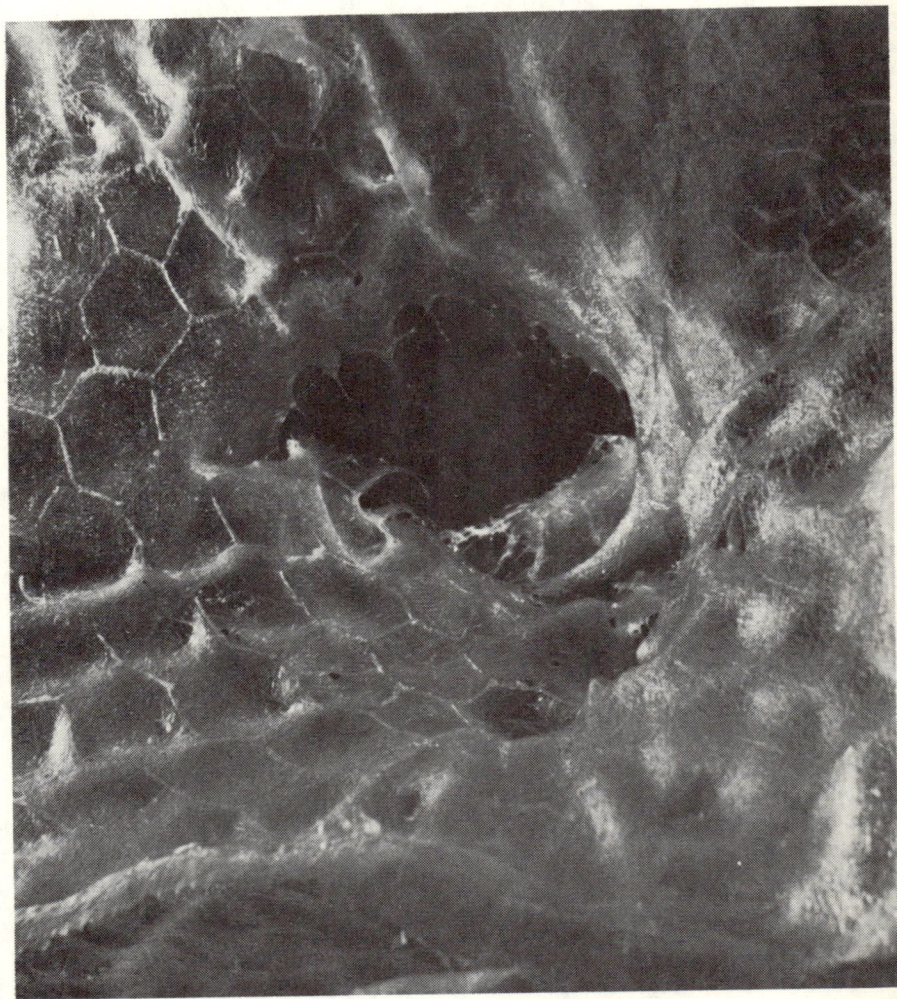

Just my two eyes
Wanting to fuse into one
And cannot shut
Even when

I shut them.

Christr Goodbye
or how we turn Christ into an 'inhuman martyr' in Belfast

i

Dandering home from work at mid
-night, they tripped Him up on a ramp,
Asked Him if He were a 'catholic' . . .

A wee bit soft in the head He was,
The last person in the world you'd want
To hurt:
              His arms and legs, broken,
His genitals roasted with a ship
-yard worker's blow lamp.

ii

In all the stories that the Christian Brothers
Tell you of Christ He never screamed
Like this. Surely this is not the way
To show a 'manly bearing'
Screaming for them to PLEASE STOP!
And then, later, like screaming for death!

When they made Him wash the stab
Wounds at the sink, they kept on
Hammering Him with the pick
-axe handle; then they pulled
Christ's trousers down, threatening to
'Cut off His balls!'

Poor boy Christ, for when
They finally got round to finishing Him off
By shooting Him in the back of the head

'The poor Fenian fucker was already dead!'

Glass Grass
for Terence Maxwell

> *'Try to*
> *Understand that you yourself*
> *are guilty of every atrocity*
> *howsoever far from you*
> *it seems to be happening.'*
> *Günter Eich*

The scorched-cloth smell and smell of burnt flesh
From morning, a bomb in one of the parked cars,
The gulls, glinting like ice on asphalt in April,
The sun, in a smog of cheap petrol exhaust
Fumes: all bring on the sinusy migraine.

Trudging against an east wind from the Cement
Factory ('awful bad for the chist!') — I wade
Through broken glass in a yellowing black smoke
Through steel-smouldering streets. There's broken glass
In my wedding shoes. (I wore them for luck!)

Ducking flying glass from the workers cleaning
Up afterwards, I take to the middle of Royal Avenue
On my way in gold rimmed polaroids to give
A poetry reading in Ballymurphy: clutching at
Ragged editions of my own poems, like clutching at

24

Strands of grass to hold you up from falling
With the crashing debris down the mountainy ware-
-houses and hotels! I promised John Hewitt and Des
Wilson, otherwise I wouldn't venture forth again
Into this too near to the knuckle disaster . . .

Tired of trying to pretend I am not this frightening
Freak has something in common with the terrorist
Of women and children, I read my poem about
The 'icons and the guns' and ask 'Now is
That "sectarian"?'
                              'We're all sectarian here!'

Some honest person replies. In the discussion after
-wards Des Wilson says 'I'm frightened of poets:
I'm frightened of their perceptions!' He wants me to answer
'Can you put yourself into the mind of the man who kills?'
'No', I lie to the priest, I can't but I can, I'm polluted

With the poison of violence, born and bred into it:
I'm dying of those dark looks I get from boy
Soldiers from slits in 'pigs' and I try to rub
The hatred from my eyes but it's deeper than 'looks':
The Black is in my lungs now, and in my poems.

My fellow poets call my poems 'cryptic, crude, dis-
-tasteful, brutal, savage, bitter . . .' and I remember
The cobbles, cluttered from broken glass, glittered
Like hailstones melting in the warm May noon, and yet
I can put myself into the mind of the man who is cold:

The rich and reverend doctors who live off the misery
Of the people like leeches, the fat-faced politicians
Grinning on TV at their own witticisms, that all
I want to do is to lie down and join the other
Grinners, grinning with horror, the skull ones,

The 'ones who died' and who are about to die.
(Here, how did all this happen inside and behind time

And why so often?) I am on the same anti-
-depressant as the back street kids and their young mothers!
On the streets again, cluttered with broken glass,

White houses, charred black, dear God! Róisín
Somebody (arrested three times by the British Army
For giving her name in Irish) drives us back
Into black smoke. Is Violet Street on fire?
We cut down across from Brian's Mini Market

Through a Crocus Street maze to the Springfield Road.
The girl I saw on Earls Court Street does not
Matter in this Barracks Defence Mechanism
Spreading its virgin male cancer cells:
A black dog, erect, a tin in its teeth

Is running between football-kicking kids
Does not see the face-fallen girl cry
Nor care. A dog has more of an in, in our very
Own BOYS' WORLD . . . A sudden black snow of
Charred newspapers, a lava of lead pencil leaves . . .

(O old ladies behind backyard walls, emptying slops
Old age 'prisoners' still watching your steps
Pray you for us 'bombs' in time-parked cars
By back-street pubs, about to burst
Into smithereens: 'fragments resulting from blows'.)

The chimney-pots flower smoke for tea time now,
And Belfast is a beaten sexless dog, hushed,
Waiting for when or where the next blow
Will fall. Against this black, the white sea-gulls
Glide in again, like hazy eyed drunks, star the dark.

Midnight Assassination

As he stares back behind the fast
-moving clouds
       at the large
Moons of childhood's
       upside down
Night field,
       all wild dais
-ey stars,
       (an odd
Light through the vest
-abule transform,
       looking up all
At once from
       putting the milk
-bottles out)
       the half-asleep,
          middle
-aged man is shot
Dead.
       Now how
         many loves
Have we lost, sharp, quick
-silver gulls,
       glinting in
The dawn-dark
     sky
       like knives?

The dead are lying dead in my gut.

Night Of The Morning
for Michael Brophy

Scurrying by our own house
Glancing at ten to twenty years
Like friends, like teeth fallen out . . .

I'm afraid to stroll down the blind
Back street I was hand-made
A mad man on. I'm afraid of
The boy (a rifle taller than himself)
Soldier lurking on the doorstep.

In this cockpit when the sun
Shifts light to the other side
I hug the in-between tide
Half-wanting to be clean done-with
The bad-cess, coming true
Dream-curse-prayer, boom
-eranging back . . .
                    Dear Ireland
One would never dream
What a night this morning has been
Like a black flag so
Delicately hovering over
The threshold of the pit
Like a child outside of our
Little town in time, crying

'Yes/No, this is my tribe,
This is my clan. By these pre-
arranged bones, I live and think,
By this skull on a stick, I am

**Womb-wall-barricaded
Bulldozed-down man.'**

Son of a Gun

'Woe to the boy
for whom the nails,
the crown of thorns,
the sponge of gall
were the first toy.'
                    François Mauriac

Between the year of the slump and the sell-out, I
The third child, am the first born alive . . .

My father is a Free Stater 'Cavan Buck'.
My mother is a Belfast factory worker. Both

Carry guns, and the grandmother with a gun
In her apron, making the Military wipe

Their boots before they rape the house. (These
Civil wars are only ever over on paper.)

Armed police are still raping my dreams
Thump-thud. Thump-thud. I go on nightmaring

Dead father running. There is a bull
In the field. Is father, am I, running away

From the bull to it? Is this the reason why
I steal time, things, places, people?

Bar-man father, sleeping with a gun under
Your pillow, does the gun help you that much I wonder

For the gun has made you all only the one
In of sex with me the two sexed son (or three

Or none) you bequeathed the gun to
Still cannot make it so. I can

Never become your he-man: shot
Down born as I was, sure, I thought

And thought and thought but blood ran . . .

The Wrong Ones

The howl of the rain beating on the military tin
Roof is like the tolling of a bell
Tolling for a childhood more
Murdering than murdered.

I rise and stalk across the scarred with storm
-erected daisies, night in the north, grass.

My water-coloured twilit-childhood island
-scape is barricaded with circles of rain-rusted
Orange, coiled to kill, barbed wire.

Behind the corrugated iron walls of the Barracks
Dead mother rises again to bang bin-lids
On dark mornings to warn husband and sons
'The Pigs, the Pigs are coming!'

The air is filled with shooting, the sky
The colour of smoke, wends across the soot
-stained grass, the grey Belfast wind
Is blowing against the unblooming-as-yet wall
-flower mind. I reach my hand out and touch
Two hundred years old iron and chipped brick.

I'll be a 'son of a gun' forever now.
Forever now I'll never be right. I'm one
Of the Wrong Ones.
                    No one will help

The rubber-bullet-collecting kids.
No one will help the grim
-faced teenaged British soldiers or young
Cops, hating the being hated.
                              We all
Go down the road now sharp and small
As razor blades . . .
                    I pick my steps across
My backstreet childhood as a soldier would pick
His steps across a little mine-filled field.

A Child Of Hatred
for John in prison

No child ought be allowed to play
Hide and Seek in these
                    'nothing but
Piles of stones'
                    where dogs dug up
The floorboards for rats
                    and soldiers
'looking guns'
                    uncover the cross
And bones of us, born and/or
Died in these wombstones
                    (until
let out) or woke while still
Alive (as if alive for gall)

And sat up and croaked a bellyfill
Of 'good-byes' all the way
From childhood:
                    the gun-toting
Monklike cops in fours patrol
By morningside dark night of

The iceberg-tip 'child soul'

Trying to hide his drinking deep

Devil white man or with him sink.

East Street

Like a young child bunged
Up with catarrh, cooing
A little teething song,
              bells, gulls,
The quiet, muffled gong
Of, as if from afar
Off, thunder of pigeons — bombs

Grind of a barrel organ, bare
Feet, cobbles . . .
'Come away from 'em other gets! You
Have shoes on *your* feet!'

Street hawkers lord it over
Children-rankled quiet in
Piercing sea-mew voices:
'Herring-a-day! Herring-a-day!'

'Any oul' scrap arn?'

'Any oul' rags for delph?'

The screeching gulls in a streaky
Bacon sky
            perch tilted
Along the pub roof drain-pipe

Wait with military eyes
For the bin men like
A house of boys
                wait their 'grub':
A silence of greed
Would waken the dead!

A dark field at the bottom of the pavings
Starred with shard upon shard
Of day-eye or sunny pee-the-bed:
Another world behind the dyke
An endless sea behind the brink of brick

Root-running,
            running,
                    down
Miles and miles below the stones
Under a boot black cloud to a
(Gas lit like moon-light)
Mud puddle and then — boom!
Another blast of pigeons.

Dark Night Of The Mill Hag

She shrieks like a bird hiccuping

'I was the Chief Bombadier . . .
We fought the Battle of Seaforde Street.
In my day I did my stint.
I organised the Turning Over of the Tram
Full of them shipyard monkeys
Coming home from holding
The heads of catholic workers
Down in the water till their lungs burst . . .

A party of a hundred women or so
Led on by myself!

Nor did we ask them to get out first!'

(On the landing, an oil lamp in her fist,
Ready to plunge the house on fire!)

'In my day there was nothing but the cream
Of Ireland's men in the IRA!
Nothing now but empty
Skites, knaves, "craters"
Leading double lives, more faces
On them than the town clock!'

She said she saw a man's head pass by
The second storey window.

'Och not a' tall gran'-ma
Or else he'd be an awful long
John Silver!'
                    Then the lamp was hurled
And geranium pot after geranium pot
Before, whoever it was, could
Find her a bed in the Asylum from
Childhood to childhood
                    in a world

-Womb to womb: to womb-removed.

The Fall

'I cling
to my sinewy
roots
are frail
I fall.'

              John Marshall

I grind teeth in my sleep.
I have worms, not light
Filtering through
Flower pot blooms . . .

An energy of hatred storms
Coursing through the blood is
What wakens me in the mornings.
It's vengeance I want
But vengeance on whom?

The brow-beaten child
Eroding on the floor
Stone with the roads
That end at the first sign
Posts run wild with dogs?

The head hanging down
To the knees is
A stone womb he tries
To hold up by the 'lugs':

'Quit screnchin!
Quit working at yerself!
Quit frownin!
Is yer head hurtin-you?'

'My head has holes inside of it.
I had a fall, I'll
Just have-to thole!

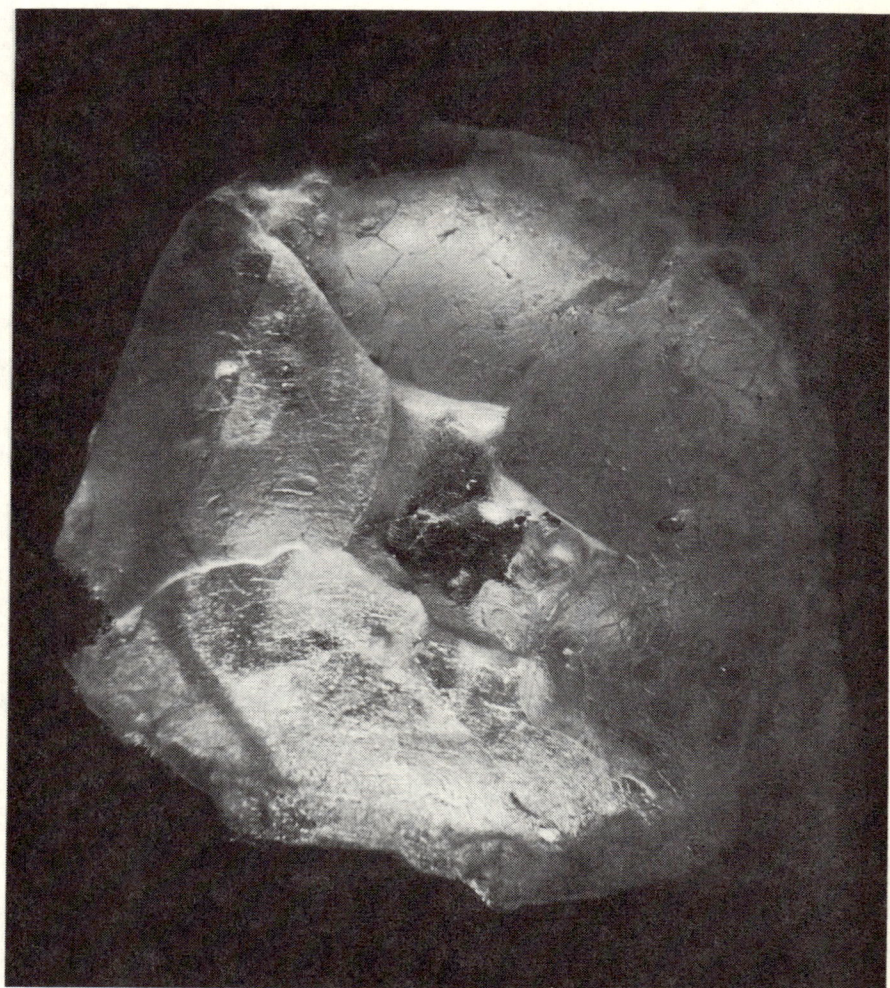

My head has holes inside of it
From being born at all.'

The Wearing Of The Black

Black velvet short trousers, the shoes
Black patent leather with crystal buttons!

'Awnnie, you have them like the Prince of Wales!'

Mother is playing 'See the Conquering Hero Comes'
And the 'Blue Bells of Scotland' on the piano.

'Where O where has my Highland Laddie gone?'

He is gone to America for
He is on the bloody run!

Our hostess, a bony whitehaired High
-land woman, brings us a cup of tea
In a rice paper thin porcelain, so
Delicate, I fumble and drop it . . .
                                    Now
Near half a century after, why
Can I recall that flash of fire
On the tile floor as I scalded my bare
Knees when I pray to care even

That this rotting self-dinner-jack-
-eted hero's grave, tonight in black
Cuff links (sparkle like hand cuffs)

At least has the wit to dress for death.

Standing Water (A Rag)

Punting into Nova Scotia
Nineteen and Twenty Nine, girl
Mother's delph face *creaks*, cracks . . .
(I'm breaking in two myself at five!)

Good-night all from the beginning.
Good-bye 'cobblestones' but
A back street womb wall won't
Let me climb out over it.

We stare at the brick Hal
-ifax sky. A yellow wolf cold
Sits on the leaden Atlantic:
A new world horizon . . . Old

Morning, you are the night of life:
The Russian Orthodox priest who
Has a beard, is the Bogey Man
Will put me in his bag

Is 'America' the Bury Hole he'll
Put me in if I cry?
On the tiny (it stops tangoing)
'transoceanic motor-ship'

Creaks, I cling hard tight onto
A Belfast flapper's strong
Wrist bone. Her stiff new
Red leather rain-coat CREAKS . . .

Our Father

Our father who art a Belfast night
-pub bouncer, had to have
A bodyguard, drilled recruits for
The IRA behind the scullery door in
The black back yard,
                    died
In your sleep, in silence like
The peasant you stayed
Never belonging on Wall Street,
Your patience a vice
Catching as a drug!
                    With no hankering
To fly back 'home', the way that you never
Left lifting your feet out of the dung
Of the fields of that crossroad town between
Leitrim, Longford and Cavan, begot
Such a high-strung, tight-knit man, but
For a drinking fit when you vented your spleen
On Heaven 'took your woman'
Hissing between nicotined teeth
Collapsing over the 'Hope Chest'
Demolishing the delph closet . . .

Bull-bellowing out in
That hollowing slum sub-way
'God damn it Christ, why,
That child belonged to me!'
                    Pray
For us now that you and she
Bed together in your American grave
At what an unnatural price
The eaten bread is soon forgotten years
Sweltering in the subway — bought
Under Mike Quill nightshift days

Hungering and agitating for
Civil Rights, a living wage
And still, still the injustices,
The evil thing being
That which crushes us . . .

To An Irish Poet Who Asked Me In French If I Were a Freak

Deprivation had my male
Elixir for a dry, white
Wine to go with your cold
Luncheon meat.
             I am full
Of hunger. You
Are full of your sold
Self, boot-licking power
Must make you hate
That which you fear —
Christ, an odd man out
Cannot be bought,
Only rented
Like the whore.

The New York Night

Hailing a cab
I black out on tar
Am slapped back awake
By cop time nagging
'Do you know who you are?'

Stupid with justice and admiration
Youth old at Grand Central Station
Light pouring down from steel beams
In this sub-way still dares dreams.

Bags which negro porters carry to
A cab set me in mind of you
Bad companions of priggish vanity
Who set me in mind of me . . .

Will it ever be different?
Horizons fawned at of male or girl
For a tiny tip, a bob twirl
Up, flip down, crown or tails?

Tails when the gamble is spent
From cold Belfast to these hell-gales.
Emerging from this air-conditioned house
Of ill-fame, I am this man, that mouse.

But who took the wind out of my sails?

London Again
for my brother, Peter, in prison

This is Cheap Side. Merchants of East
End lay down their rugs at

Market Stall, light years from 'home':
Great peoples sunk low to the pawns!

Me, the most important, now the least
Redundant in the alley of any ghetto rat

Throbs a salted open freak on the roam
Through wilderness of densities to dawns

Smoggy at the vague marshes at the knark
                              of light . . .

'Don't shelter him, don't have any
Thing to do with him' is perfectly right.

I who dart, day by day, through lit night
Under wharf sewer with holes in beads
                              for eyes

Would not give my brother gun-man a penny
For fear he'd begin to look for skies

To glut down to slot machines and stir

Reminiscences of sheer
Uncontaminated air . . .

Sermon To Us Ghetto Rats

detective apprehending young English
Negro from stowing away on the night-boat:
'There's no such a place as Africa!
That boat's going to Belfast!'

'Lucky', Alun Owen

Born unfixed to bend and break
And leave behind
No gain in going, no take
In staying still and cannot sleep
All dead men wake

Again, the bone gone on
By being left behind
Is blotted out by light,
We grow into some strange
Unknown 'other one' . . .

Eyes in back of the head
Be whispering despair, afraid
Of the bomb in the public.house
You'd disappear
Each from the other in
-to anywhere . . .

Suits the child-wanderer of us
Who once had been that intimate
(if self-devoured children left
Like a pattern on the plate
But because together make
The 'crucified'
Must grow from the one another by
A process of decay
Lovers learn to hate
Then to obey) . . .

You go, I go, good
-bye, our fate
Never belongs to us
Alone, always to others.

The Let Hell Go Of It
for Tom Kilroy

After I helped you tear up
The gangplank from the Law
As I mounted the bus back

Into town, and my old umbrella
Cracked from an ice-storm wind our
'old acquaintanceship', I

Gaped at and prayed to the driver
'It would be a good idea' he swore
'to let friggin go-of-it!'

Yes, day is night out in
The hailstone skinning sky
As I watch my broken stick

(All spokes) — fly
Down the whimpering street,
Your liner far out into

The bitch Atlantic now:
An elongated neck of the snow
Goose in flight ship-horn

Honk of the cow in heat,
An art-long, ram-rod flicker
Of fingers, then: GONE!

Well then, good, great, I love
You all the more because
You are not here . . .

Credo Credo
for Aidan and Aine

You soldiers who make for our holy
Pictures, grinding the glass with your
Rifle butts, kicking and jumping on them

With your hob-nailed boots, we
Are a richer dark than the Military
Machine could impose ever.

We have the ancient, hag-ridden, long
In the tooth Mother, with her ugly
Jewish Child

Hangs in the depths of our dark
Secret being, no rifles can reach
Nor bullets, nor boots:

It was our icons not our guns
You spat on. When you found our guns
You got down on your knees to them

As if our guns were the holy thing . . .
And even should you shoot the swarthy
-faced Mother with her ugly Jewish Child

Who bleeds with the people, she'll win
Because she loses all with the people,
Has lost every war for centuries with us.

Soldiers
for Seamus Deane

The altar boy marches up the altar steps.
The priest marches down. 'Get up now
And be a soldier!' says the nun
To the woman after giving birth, 'Get up now
And march, march: Be a man!'

And the men are men and the women are men
And the children are men!

Mother carried a knife to work.
It was the thorn to her rose . . .

They say she died with her eyes open
In the French Hospital in New York.
I remember those eyes shining in the dark

Slum hallway the day after
I left the monastery: Eyes that were
A feast of welcome that said 'Yes,
I'm glad you didn't stay stuck there!'

'Would you mind if I went to prison
Rather than war?'
'No, for Ireland's men all went to prison!'

At the bottom of a canyon of brick
She cursed and swore
'You never see the sky!'

A lifetime after,
                just before
I go to sleep at night, I hear
That Anna Magnani voice screaming
Me deaf 'No! No, you're not
To heed the world!' In one swift
Sentence she tells me not to yield
But to *forbear*:
                'Go to prison but never
Never stop fighting. We are the poor
And the poor have to be "soldiers".

You're still a soldier, it's only that
You're losing the war

And all the wars are lost anyway!'

The Ditch Of Dawn

In memory of my dear friend,
Gerry McLaughlin,
murdered 7 April 1975

How I admired your bravado
Dandering down the road alone
In the dark yelling, 'I'll see
You again, tomorrow', but

They pumped six bullets into you.

Now you are lying in a mud
Puddle of blood, yelling
Through the stars

There's no 'Good-bye',
No 'Safe Home' in
This coffin country where
Your hands are clawed . . .

(How can I tell anyone here
i'm born, born lying in
This ditch of a cold Belfast dawn
With the bullet mangled body of
A dead boy
                and can't
Can't get away?)
                A young
British soldier wanders
Over to my old
                donkey honk
Of bitter *Miserere* of
Dereliction on the street:

'What is it mate, what is it?

WHAT'S WRONG?'